U.S. GOVERNMENTAL INFORMATION OPERATIONS AND STRATEGIC COMMUNICATIONS: A DISCREDITED TOOL OR USER FAILURE? IMPLICATIONS FOR FUTURE CONFLICT

Do not believe what you want to believe until you know what you ought to know.

> Professor R. V. Jones
> Principal Scientific Advisor
> United Kingdom Secret
> Intelligence Service

BACKGROUND

In the two wars of choice that have defined the first decade of the 21st century, the United States and its coalition partners have found that despite overwhelming supremacy of firepower, the digitization of the battlefield, exceptional Intelligence, Surveillance, Targeting and Reconnaissance (ISTAR) capabilities, advanced cyber and other agency assistance, and an unsophisticated and often disparate enemy, the concept of "victory" has remained stubbornly elusive. In Iraq, despite massive investment of blood and treasure by both the United States and its coalition partners, the turning point was arrived at not simply as a result of a troop surge, but through unanticipated events among the local population.[1] In Afghanistan, a seemingly beaten homogenous enemy slowly returned to battle, morphing into a more heterogeneous group, picking the time and place of their engagement and utilizing cheap yet deadly effective weaponry such as improvised explosive devices (IEDs) to cause significant damage to coalition personnel, materiel, and mo-

1

rale, before slipping back into the communities from which they are drawn.

Alongside this hard-won experience from the ground, significant academic and doctrinal research has suggested that the United States and its allies may actually have approached their campaigns in the wrong way. For example, in *War By Other Means*, RAND suggested that:

> The existence of a global Muslim community that has a personality in the world arena challenges the U.S. strategic concept of a war on terror that narrowly seeks military outcomes while ignoring the hostility it may engender in that larger community. Lost in the fog of GWOT [Global War on Terrorism] is whether using armies to fight terrorists hidden among Muslim populations is spawning more hostility and resistance. The data suggest that it is.[2]

RAND was not alone. Books such as John MacKinlay's *Insurgent Archipelago*,[3] which warns of the "propaganda of the deed," David Kilcullen's *Accidental Guerilla*,[4] and General Rupert Smith's *The Utility of Force*[5] all point to the need for a different campaign strategy for the wars of the 21st century. A critical mass of policy and doctrine maker's opinion slowly formed, and the United States and its allies have started looking at other ways of achieving effect. A very visible demonstration of this was the establishment and deployment of Human Terrain Teams (HTT) designed to provide specialist social science and anthropological analysis to deployed commanders, a program which owes its lineage to the U.S. Civil Operations and Revolutionary Development Support (CORDS), a counterinsurgency (COIN) program developed by the U.S. Government during the Vietnam war.[6] However, there have been developments in COIN doctrine that have, perhaps, most clearly signposted the change in thinking, alongside the traditional emphasis on the importance of "hearts and minds," a new awareness of the global information space and a commensurate expansion of activities often defined as "soft" (i.e., invariably non-kinetic in nature and clearly delineated from the more traditional application of controlled violence by military forces). A new and often confusing lexicon has simultaneously grown, with terms such as "strategic communication" and "influence" rising to prominence.

These developments have not been without controversy. Both within the military establishment and outside of it, there have been notable critics. U.S. military academic Colonel (Retired) Gian Gentile wrote in *Small Wars Journal*: "We are placing the cart of **convincing** [soft effects] before the horse of **killing** [hard effects] and in so doing we are quickly losing our way as an Army of the free world,"[7] while Lieutenant Colonel (Retired) John L. Cook, U.S. Army, wrote:

> The strategy being employed by the coalition places a higher value on the lives of Afghan civilians than the lives of American soldiers—these are the rules of engagement designed to win the hearts and minds of the Afghan civilians.[8]

The media, too, have been highly critical of the manner in which soft effects had been pursued. Tom Vanden Brook of the *USA Today* newspaper is a long standing critic of the Department of Defense (DoD) Informational Operations (IO) efforts. In February 2012, he published an investigative article about the cost of U.S. IO writing that:

From 2005 to 2009, such spending rose from $9 million to $580 million a year mostly in Iraq [as] Afghanistan, Pentagon and congressional records show. . . . A USA TODAY investigation, based on dozens of interviews and a series of internal military reports, shows that Pentagon officials have little proof the programs work and they won't make public where the money goes.[9]

In November 2012, in the same paper, he wrote:

Since 2000, the military has paid The Rendon Group more than $100 million to help shape its communications strategy, analyze media coverage, run its propaganda programs, and develop counter-narcotics efforts around the world.[10]

Vanden Brook went on to quote U.S. Army Colonel Paul Yingling, who served three tours in Iraq between 2003 and 2009 as an IO specialist, as describing IO at the time as "doing posters, fliers or radio ads. These things are unserious."[11]

Because of his persistently critical coverage, Vanden Brook's reporting is often dismissed by the DoD's IO community, however, there have also been some officially sponsored studies that have appeared to echo at least some of his criticism. In May 2012, for example, RAND published *US Military Information Operations In Afghanistan: Effectiveness of Psychological Operations 2001-2010*,"[12] a report commissioned by the U.S. Marine Corps (USMC). This paper's single most important conclusion was that:

. . . if the overall Information Operation (IO) mission in Afghanistan is defined as convincing most residents of contested areas to side decisively with the Afghan government and its foreign allies against the Taliban insurgency, this has not been achieved.

4

This came just a year after the U.S. House Appropriations Committee had threatened to deduct $125 million from the $300 million that was being sought in the 2012 Defense Appropriations Bill for Military Information Support Operations (MISO) support. Realistically, this was probably never a serious threat, more an internal "red flag" to DoD and MISO communities, drawing attention to what many were concerned was a potentially failing enterprise and which Congress feared was lacking proper oversight and accountability.

Soon after, and with perhaps unfortunate timing, an unrelated and later regretted public proclamation that strategic communication was ending burst onto the scene in the so called "Little Memo"[13] written by George Little, Assistant to the Secretary for Defense for Public Affairs. This publicly (and apparently unilaterally) stated that strategic communication added a "layer of staffing and planning that blurred the roles and functions of traditional staff elements and blurred understanding . . . as a result of this we stood down these staff elements." Commentators from across the IO community responded unhappily to the memo on message boards and blogs. From the U.S. Joint Information Operations Warfare Center (JIOWC), Richard Josten declared on the Strategic Communication forum of LinkedIn that:

> Many of the problems associated with Strategic Communication come from the term itself. Too many consider it to be about marketing and too many consider it to be about communications with an 'S'.[14]

Senior DoD official and former journalist Rosa Brooks, in her public response to the memo, stated that:

> . . . this latest memo is just another shot fired in the ongoing skirmish between those who believe that strategic communication is merely an unnecessary euphemism for 'communications' — meaning, basically, press statements and talking points — and thus should be controlled by public affairs offices, and those who believe strategic communication is a confusing term, but one that has nonetheless come to stand for something complex and important, something that has more to do with strategy than with communications.[15]

Mark Laity, Chief of Strategic Communications (SC) at North Atlantic Treaty Organization (NATO) Supreme Headquarters Allied Powers Europe (SHAPE) wrote that:

> It has taken us huge amounts of effort to get nearly 30 NATO nations [to] agree to a policy, and for years we've been out there arguing for and explaining the Strategic Communication mindset. Now I'm meant to say, 'Hey Heads of State, me and the guys have been chatting and think we should change the name.' The term is bigger than us, the clean piece of paper has writing scrawled all over it. Changing the name just hits the reset button and we start all over. The new 'communication synchronization' highlights the danger of meddling with the term — Little introduced it precisely to kill Strategic Communication. It's a narrow, limited, un-ambitious phrase intended to redefine and belittle what Strategic Communication did/ does in order to say it's not needed.[16]

With the cessation of operations in Afghanistan imminent but still no clear outcome apparent, the outside observer might be forgiven for thinking that U.S.

governmental SC efforts, and in particular DoD IO, are under some form of existential stress. The fortunes of U.S. IO and SC are inextricably linked to those of other NATO nations, and it is with some concern, although perhaps not surprise, that these events have been viewed from other capitals, specifically London, England; Canberra, Australia; and the NATO headquarters in Brussels, Belgium, with deep concern. For those in the wider global SC and IO communities engaged in the same war of ideas as the United States, the idea of America sneezing and Europe catching a cold, a rather over-used if still apt metaphor, has never been more important.

THE TYRANNY OF TERMINOLOGY

One of the inhibitors to nuanced discussion about this subject is the tyranny of terminology — the large number of new terms and definitions, often used interchangeably, that have arisen since 2001. For the purposes of this monograph, the following terminology is used; where not otherwise stated, the definitions are the author's own.

Information Operations.

US DoD *Joint Publication (JP) 3-13, Information Operations,*[17] defines IO as integrated employment during military operations of information related capabilities (IRCs) in concert with other lines of operation to influence, disrupt, corrupt, or usurp the decisionmaking of adversaries and potential adversaries while protecting our own capabilities.

Military Information Support Operations.

JP 3-13 defines MISO as planned operations to convey selected information and indicators to foreign audiences to influence their emotions, motives, objective reasoning, and ultimately the behavior of foreign governments, organizations, groups, and individuals in a manner favorable to the originator's objectives. In the rest of NATO, this function is still referred to by its former name, Psychological Operations (PsyOps).

Target Audience Analysis.

Target Audience Analysis (TAA) is an empirical process in which the motivations for specific group behavior are analyzed, using qualitative and quantitative research methods.

Influence.

(noun): the inherent understanding that all Diplomatic, Information, Military & Economic (DIME) activities have the potential to influence the behaviors and attitudes of specific groups.
(verb): the application of specific activities to a target audience to influence behaviors and attitudes.
(It should be noted that U.S. DoD *Field Manual (FM) 3-13, Inform and Influence Activities,* issued January 2013, has now specifically removed a doctrinal definition of "influence" per se but offers an explanation of what it might constitute:

> Influence activities typically focus on persuading selected foreign audiences to support US objectives or to persuade those audiences to stop supporting the adversary or enemy.

Strategic Communication.

U.S. JP 1-02[18] defines SC as focused U.S. Government efforts to understand and engage key audiences to create, strengthen, or preserve conditions favorable for the advancement of U.S. Government interests, policies, and objectives through the use of coordinated programs, plans, themes, messages, and products synchronized with the actions of all instruments of national power.

In previous iterations of U.S. IO doctrine, IRCs were specifically named. These were Operational Security (OPSEC), Military Deception (MILDEC), Electronic Warfare (EW), and Computer Network Operations (CNO). However, all of these fall well beyond the threshold for unclassified discussion and, while there can be no debate about their relevance on the operational field of battle, it is more debatable how they directly contribute (with the exception of CNO) to U.S. SC efforts and therefore will not be discussed here. So, too, Public Affairs, which, while clearly a key element of SC, is mainly concerned with "informing" audiences, and typically domestic ones at that. Therefore, this monograph will focus its analysis on MISO/PsyOps, which, as noted by FM 3-13, is the commanders "primary capability to influence **foreign** populations in the areas of operations" in order to "persuade selected foreign audiences to support US objectives or to persuade those audiences to stop supporting the adversary or enemy." That analysis must begin with a brief critique of past performance and three case studies, two from Afghanistan and the other from Pakistan.

CASE STUDY 1 - AFGHANISTAN

In November 2011, the author attended a meeting in International Security and Assistance Force (ISAF) Headquarters (HQ) in Kabul, Afghanistan, to discuss a possible information operation to reduce the number of young men of fighting age who were joining the insurgency. The pilot plan, to pay young Afghan men of fighting age in certain provinces a wedding dowry of up to $6,000, had been introduced by a contractor to a senior U.S. flag officer. In a clever coup, it appeared to the inexperienced (in IO matters) general that ISAF would take huge swathes of fighters off the battlefield by facilitating their marriages to eligible young Afghan women. All it took was money—and lots of it. The plan, presented by the International Council on Security and Development (ICOS) promised four outcomes from the plan:

1. To identify those individuals who are the most vulnerable socially, and prevented from marrying due to lack of financial resources;

2. To test the receptiveness of the local population towards the program;

3. To identify mechanisms for preventing fraud in delivering the grants; and,

4. To evaluate the effectiveness of the project, as measured by a change of attitudes of program participants regarding their role in the community.

The author was asked to evaluate the plan. The first objection was money: The author demonstrated to the command that the cost of the program (from the 150-person pilot through to all eligible Helmandi males and then on across the country) would quickly exceed U.S.$4 billion per year. A number of other problems were also identified. First, the plan was based on the assumption that married men would be less inclined to join the insurgency; yet the marital status of most of the detainees held in coalition detention facilities suggested this assumption was not valid. Second, according to the contractor, the measure of effect of the program would be a change in attitudes. As shown later, attitudes are highly temporal and are all but impossible to measure accurately. Were I an Afghan male who had just been given $6000, I would undoubtedly be hugely grateful. But for how long and to what effect? But what if I was were an Afghan male who had not been given the $6000? The prospect of this last factor was of most concern, for it would see huge injections of unearned cash into small micro-communities, with all the attendant second- and third-order effects that would inevitably follow: corruption, jealousy, and feuds. In summarizing the assessment of the plan, this author was compelled to write that:

> . . . there is no empirical research to suggest that this is a sensible solution to deterring young men of fighting age from joining the insurgency. Even if there were, it would be cost prohibitive and open to such widespread and pernicious abuse as to render it unworkable.[19]

It was quite clear from the stony-faced reaction of the general and the urgent protestations of the contractor that this was not the answer desired. Fortunately, several weeks later, wiser heads prevailed, and the program was cancelled on the grounds of cost, if none of the other attendant issues.

CASE STUDY 2 - PAKISTAN

In September 2012, the U.S. Government purchased advertising slots on Pakistani national television to denounce the controversial and offensive anti-Islamic video, *The Innocence of Muslims*, featuring the prophet Mohammed. This initiative followed huge demonstrations near the U.S. Embassy in Islamabad, and outbreaks of anti-American violence elsewhere including the murder of the U.S. Ambassador to Libya, Christopher Stevens. The advertisement included statements by President Barack Obama and then Secretary of State Hillary Clinton criticizing the film.

The advertising campaign bore a striking resemblance to a previous U.S. communication campaign run by commercial marketer Charlotte Beers. Beers was the instigator of a $15 million marketing campaign entitled "Shared Values," which, following the September 11, 2001 (9/11) attacks, produced a series of TV advertisements depicting the daily lives of U.S. Muslims. The program was launched in Indonesia, the world's most populous Muslim country, but failed to find outlets in the Middle East; many in the Arab world belittled the campaign as simple-minded and condescending. Media reports both abroad and in the United States were generally negative, and the project was widely viewed as crude propaganda. Both *CNN* and *The Wall Street Journal* reported that the initiative had totally failed to connect with Muslim audiences. Beers was more upbeat, claiming that the campaign had been successful because it had started a dialogue. No formal quantitative evaluation of the campaign was ever made public, which perhaps in itself calls into question the optimistic interpretation of its achievements. In March 2003, Beers resigned from the

State Department, and the project collapsed. Given the similarity between the 2012 TV advertisements and the Beers' campaign, it would appear the ideas behind it did not collapse.

In assessing the Pakistan TV advertisements, a number of questions arise, chiefly about accessibility and reach. First, of the large body of people who chose to riot, probably only a very tiny percentage had actually seen the offending video. The video is 74 minutes in duration and a little over 400-megabytes (MB) in size. "Highlights" could therefore have been available to smart phones, but it would be next to impossible to view properly without access to the web. While Internet penetration in Pakistan is undeniably growing, literacy in Pakistan is still less than 55 percent, and around 30 to 40 percent of the population live beneath the poverty line, which suggests limited access to the Internet via computer. At the same time, viewing the U.S. response required both access to a TV set and the ability either to understand English or to read the superimposed Urdu script. It is a reasonable supposition, therefore, that many of the rioters had probably never seen the original video, nor the presidential address that followed, and that their knowledge of its existence was largely second hand, transmitted through trusted community leaders and/or social networks such as mosques.

Secondly, the anger over the video was all the more intense because it aligned with the ongoing manifestation of the wider and very long-standing "*U.S. hates Muslims*" narrative. It joined an already long list of perceived injustices, including the Palestine Iraq, and Afghanistan conflicts, as well as the past desecration of Korans. In this context, it seems optimistic that a few words in a TV advertisement from the U.S. President, the embodiment of the western "infidel," could appease an enraged mob.

Third, the objective of the advertisements was ostensibly to reduce undesired behavior. The President stated in the advertisement that the video did not reflect U.S. views or U.S. policy. He further stated that the United States respected the Islamic religion and Muslims. In short, the President sought to change people's attitudes toward the United States in the hope that their behavior, the rioting, would stop. Given the widespread acceptance of the "*U.S. hates Muslims*" narrative that pervades the Islamic world, this appears ambitious. More relevantly, it ignored a considerable body of social science research accrued over many years which indicates that attitudes are not strong precursors to behavioral change. Achieving an understanding of how to mitigate and reduce behavior is extremely difficult.

The advertisements were not, of course, the sole U.S. response to the video. Ever since President Obama's 2009 "New Beginning" speech in Cairo, Egypt, the United States has been trying to rebuild its image in the Arab and Muslim world. However, the advertising campaign did cost the U.S. taxpayer significant amounts of money, and, yet it can be argued that from the outset, the chances of success were debatable. Indeed, subsequently ABC news reported on September 21, 2012, that:

> Deadly anti-U.S. protests erupted in Pakistan despite an unusual ad on Pakistani TV featuring President Obama and Secretary of State Hillary Clinton denouncing the movie *Innocence of Muslims*, the anti-Islam video that has fueled much of the Pakistani fury. The ads have been running this week on seven different Pakistani television stations in an attempt to

cool tempers over the film, but today's protests were the largest seen so far since the controversy began in Pakistan last week with the attempted storming of the US embassy.[20]

Neither of the preceding case studies is intended to belittle U.S. attempts — indeed, far from it. Unlike many other countries, the United States is at least prepared to take risks and attempt new ideas. But both demonstrate very starkly the difficulties that have beset the United States in the past 12 years: susceptibility to ambitious contractors, an absence of "intelligent customers,"[21] and an apparent absence of understanding how communication can, and cannot, be realistically employed to mitigate crisis and conflict.

CASE STUDY 3 - AFGHANISTAN

What might proper behaviorally-based campaigns in Afghanistan have looked like? In April 2011, the author toured ISAF HQ in Kabul, offering up nine behavioral campaigns to meet immediate operational problems. One, designed to improve retention in the Afghanistan National Security Forces (ANSF), is summarized here.

Background.

ISAF will struggle to build the ANSF the country needs with current retention rates. Lieutenant General William Caldwell has stated that "based on current attrition rates, to expand security forces by 56,000, we will need to recruit 133,000."[22]

Methodology.

First, undertake qualitative and quantitative TAA to determine the facts that influence ANSF leaving what are, for Afghan society, well-paid jobs. Second, instigate behavioral interventions to increase retention. In order to complete these tasks, it will be necessary to interview serving ANSF, those who have already left and the communities from which they are drawn.

Costs.

600 Quantitative questionnaires per district. Unit cost $30.	$90,000
80 Qualitative interviews per district. Total 400. Unit cost of $334	$133,600
2 focus group discussions per district. Total 10. Unit cost of $3,340	$33,400
10 Subject Matter Expert interviews per district. Unit cost $334	$16,700
Data analysis and production of influence plan	$250,000
Total cost of analysis	$557,780

Timing.

The TAA process will take approximately 3 months, the analysis approximately 2 months. The influence program will extend over 18 months, with first measures of effectiveness (MOE) being made available at the 12-month point.

Deliverables.

The program is divided into three parts. The TAA and Influence Intervention plan are provided by contractors. The influence intervention is undertaken by NATO Training Mission-Afghanistan (NTM[A]) with ISAF Combined Joint Psychological Operations Task Force (CJPOTF) support.

Proposed Behavioral Program.

The other behaviorally based programs suggested included disruption of the narcotics supply chain, promotion of alternative livelihoods, and increased Pashtun recruiting into the ANSF. In total, each behavioral campaign cost approximately $500,000, a tiny amount in comparison to the estimated $3.6 billion a month[23] that the United States has been spending in Afghanistan and the multi-million dollar contracts awarded to contractors for attitudinal marketing campaigns.

What was remarkable about the proposed behavioral program was that it met with universal acceptance across the ISAF military community as a worthwhile idea, and yet never happened. A great many other companies have contractors embedded in the U.S. and ISAF command chains—it failed to pass their scrutiny. Other explanations for this failure included the following:

1. This program was not the invention of the contracting companies, and neither would they be generating revenue by running it;

2. The final results of the program would not be known for at least 12 months—in other words, after most people involved had left the theater; and,

17

3. The weight of ISAF bureaucracy required a program of this nature to be fully costed, tendered, evaluated, and approved years ahead in order to meet the requirements of budgets and resource accounting.

What is demonstrated by these three case studies is that the implementation, or otherwise, of an IO program, as with much else in western militaries and governments, can depend less on its assessed outcome than on expediency, bureaucracy, and vested interests. The remainder of this monogram proposes a means of mitigating this situation.

THE SCIENCE OF COMMUNICATION

Despite the enormous number of theories seeking to explain the nature of human communication, most broadly agree that communication, whatever its form, is designed to be either informative or persuasive, or a synergy of the two. For example, a roadside speed sign is designed to inform drivers of the local vehicle speed limit and, by implication, encourage them to abide by it. While many people may obey the sign, particularly if it is supplemented by the additional detail of a school or playground being close by (thus providing a rationale for the limit), many others may not. Their conformity might, however, be ensured if there is a speed camera present—their behavior now moderated not by concern for pedestrians, but by the threat of a speeding ticket and/or fine.

In the United Kingdom (UK), there has been a concerted move over recent decades to reduce traffic speed limits to 20 miles per hour in built-up areas. Yet, where this has occurred, the accident rate, perhaps counterintuitively, has actually gone up. According to the UK's Department of Transport,[24] this is because motorists have become frustrated with the slow pace of travel, while at the same time, pedestrians have become complacent and have not paid necessary attention to the traffic. It is only where speed cameras have been installed that accident rates have actually gone down. So we can conclude from this very simple example that attitudinal and informational communication (the speed restriction signs) may work with some people but cannot be guaranteed for the majority of the people. Indeed, there may well be second- and third-order effects of this communication that were never considered or anticipated—in this example, pedestrians becoming complacent and drivers angry. This vignette shows that even in the simplest cases, communication is by no means an easy subject to understand.

Long experience of communicating in crisis and conflict environments has shown that three broad types of communication products are deployed through MISO activity: Informational, Attitudinal, and Behavioral. Understanding how each is used to best advantage is seminal to understanding why U.S. communication efforts have been so problematic in the wars since 2001. This understanding is not helped by a considerable amount of academic literature providing often conflicting advice and guidance. Take, for example, RAND's 2005 study: *Dissuading Terror. Strategic Influence and Struggle against Terrorism* [sic]. The paper's authors declare that:

> influence campaigns can produce a variety of real-world behaviors . . . . But before an operation can produce these behaviors it must first alter the target audiences' attitudes, opinions, reasoning and/or emotions.[25]

Yet this would appear to be diametrically at odds with the conclusions of a 2010 paper by Professors William Hutchinson and Mathew Warren, *Influence Operations and Behavioural Change.* This paper asserts that the relationship between attitudes and behaviors is "challenging" and that "evidence showing [that] attitudes lead to behaviors is weak, whereas evidence showing [that] behaviour leads to attitudes is stronger."[26] With such apparent confusion over what should be targeted, it is perhaps understandable that the United States might question the very worth of such programs. However, it is this author's view that understanding how each is used to its best advantage is seminal to understanding why U.S. communication and wider ISAF efforts have been so problematic in Afghanistan and is key to their employment in future conflict.

Informational Communication.

As the name suggests, informational communication conveys a piece of information from a source to an audience that may not previously have been known. In the context of military operations in Afghanistan, informational communication is regularly deployed. For example, ISAF may wish to explain to local Afghans why a forward operating base (FOB) is being expanded or reduced; why military vehicles should not be tailgated by civilian cars; of new school or community reconstruction projects being undertaken in the area; or, indeed, of the telephone number for the confidential telephone Tip Line to report insurgent activities. All are perfectly valid and fall within the NATO definition of PsyOps/MISO: truthful and attributable activity directed at an approved target audience. A good example of an informational poster, albeit one designed to elicit a behavioral response, was produced but never deployed by British Forces in Afghanistan in July 2011 when a British soldier went missing (see Figure 1).[27] The poster informed the local population that a British serviceman was missing and what he would look like. The audience's attention is brought to the 110 Confidential Tip Line. Clearly, this poster is designed to encourage behavior (to find the missing serviceman), but, at its heart, it is informational, not least as the area in which the soldier was missing was immediately flooded with ISAF troops and the local populace would have been puzzled, perhaps even concerned, at their presence.

Figure 1. British Missing Soldier.

Informational Communication is a vital component in a COIN environment, particularly one in which the insurgent will take every opportunity to twist the interpretation of events to his advantage. The insurgent, typically, is unconcerned with either accuracy or veracity of message, while, for COIN operatives, there are conflicting imperatives being first with the truth while balancing the need to constantly and promptly keep the contested population abreast of current events.

Attitudinal Communication.

This type of communication seeks to either reinforce positive attitudes or dislodge negative attitudes in discrete target audiences. In NATO's mission to Afghanistan, it is perhaps best exemplified by the twin and long standing projects of roadside billboards and newspapers. Across Afghanistan, there are some 296 centrally funded billboards, maintained at a cost of U.S.$4.9 million per year, which are used to promote the government of Afghanistan and the notion of "good" governance. However, this centrally funded figure is just the tip of the iceberg; in Wardak and Logar provinces, for example, there were 150 different billboards paid for by at least four separate DoD actors in 2009-10; so too in Helmand and Kandahar, all created, printed, and maintained at considerable expense. At the same time ISAF produces a newspaper entitled *Sada-e Azadi*[28] which, in three languages, seeks to present to literate Afghans a post-insurgency view of their country in a magazine format. The image shown in Figure 2 is an example of an attitudinal type PsyOps leaflet. A soldier of the Afghan National Army (ANA), and two policemen, one from the Afghan National Police (ANP) and one from the Afghan Local Police (ALP) are shown side by side, the reassuring message beneath suggesting that they all have a common aim for the benefit of the populace. Clearly there is an implicit behavior encouraged by this poster—"support the organs of organic Afghan security, not the Taliban."

Figure 2. ANP, ANA, and ALP Attitudes.

Another example is this roadside poster in Helmand. (See Figure 3.) The poster reads: "Poppy. Poppy is damaging the Pashtun's house, country, community and future generations. What do you think? Contact us on this number." This is clearly designed to change attitudes and encourage debate that will ultimately lead to the demise of poppy cultivation—a key wish for the international community. Yet it might be argued that far from "damaging the Pashtun's house," poppy shores it up by being extremely profitable, providing a source of income to farmers that they would not be able to derive from vegetables, fruit, and wheat. Indeed, Lieutenant Colonel (Retired) John L. Cook believes that in Helmand and Kandahar: "The poppy is king providing, either directly or indirectly, nearly 80% of all jobs in these provinces."[29]

Figure 3. Roadside Poppy Poster.

In many areas of Afghanistan, the poppy poster may be a message that resonates with Afghans, but this is certainly not a uniform response, and neither is the response to the previous example highlighting the ANSF. Thus we can suggest, with some confidence, that this type of attitudinal product depends heavily upon the temporal circumstances of the audience. They may have had good experiences of the police and feel reassured by the poster. They may think poppy cultivation is wrong and want to do something about it. Alternatively, they may have had poor experiences with the police, or they may make a healthy yearly profit from opium production. In these circumstances, the posters would seem irrelevant and detract from the credibility of the Afghan government rather than enhancing it.

Behavioral Communication.

This type of communication is seen as the "Holy Grail" of IO, and, in many instances, seems just as elusive. Behavioral communication is completely focused on mitigating or encouraging specific and pre-determined behaviors. For example, a MISO campaign may be used to directly target the trafficking of drugs, or to boost retention among the Afghan National Army. However, behavioral communication can also be surprisingly effective in changing attitudes, particularly when they are deployed subtly and with discretion. Attitudinal communication is invariably obvious, "in your face," and its intent also obvious—it can be quickly discarded as mere propaganda. Nuanced behavioral campaigns cannot be so discarded. This stratagem was utilized to great effect during, for example, President Barack Obama's "Change" campaign. Working closely with behavioral psychologists, the campaign team generated a social media "viral" meme that aimed to excite people into turning up at Obama's rallies. It worked by suggesting to locals that record numbers of supporters were to turn up, and it would be an incredible spectacle to behold. The idea behind this approach was that the very act of attending the rallies—even for non-Obama supporters and fence-sitters—would be so emotionally arousing and stimulating that people would form fresh positive attitudes towards Obama, and subsequently vote for him. The resulting election results bear testament to the idea's validity.

In truth the invented term "behavioral communication" is a slight misnomer. As we have seen, attitudinal and informational communication can have both implicit and explicit behavioral consequences—although, as will be demonstrated in a moment, the perceived wisdom that attitudes lead directly to behaviors is not borne out in scientific studies, indeed, just the opposite. So it is not so much "behavioral communication" as a discreet term that is deployed, but activities and actions in support of specific behavioral objectives, and as this monograph will show, has for a very long time been secondary in U.S. thinking and practice to mitigating and changing people's attitudes and perceptions.

This monograph suggests that imperfect understanding of the different types of communication and their likely outcome lies at the root of U.S. and wider Western failure in prosecuting IO. The naïve and unquestioning implementation of TV campaigns such as the Pakistani TV advertisements described earlier is costly, especially given that the impact or effect sought—behavioral change—is so uncertain. It is this author's view that, in any conflict environment, it is

the physical behavior of different groups that determine outcomes. Yet, it would appear that the bulk of
effort and expenditure to date has been directed at attitudinal communications in the hope that they will
engender positive behavioral change. Indeed, detailed
reading of U.S. and wider NATO doctrine reveals that
the focus of activity is still the communication of information and messages (and hence a focus upon
attitudes). For example, the newly released FM 3-13
provides nearly two pages of guidance (pp. 1.3-1.5)
on messaging, provides a message development flow-
chart that is entirely top-down and without any reference to the proposed audience. Or put another way,
it is entirely sender oriented with a presumption that
the message will get through if you just transmit it in
the right way. This is often referred to as the "mes-
sage-influence" model and may be represented as
in Figure 4.

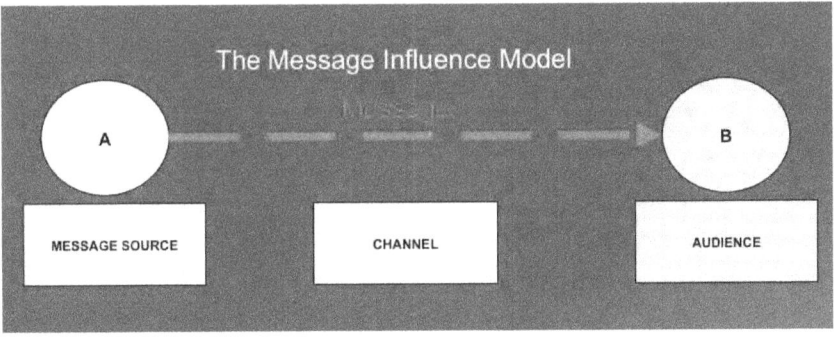

Figure 4. The Message Influence Model.

However, we know even from our own interper-
sonal communication that this is a far too simplistic
model, that there are significant factors that might
complicate and corrupt the message. The Center for

Strategic Communication at Arizona State University published a detailed study of these complicating factors in 2008 entitled *Strategic Communication on a Rugged Landscape*.[30] Like many other studies, they demonstrated that the message sent very often was not the message received, its receipt and understanding being heavily contextualized by background attitudes and perceptions. (See Figure 5.)

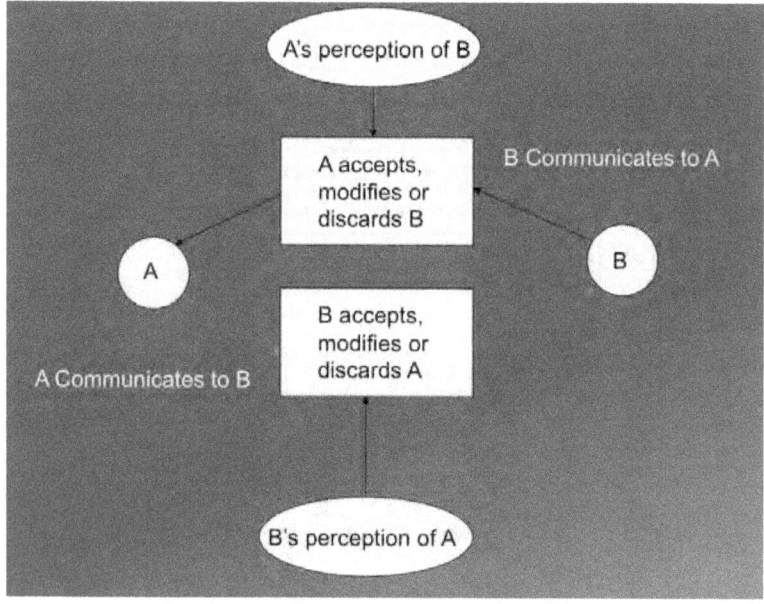

Figure 5. Pragmatic Communication Model.

It is rare to hear senior officers talk of **behaviors** but exceptionally common to hear discussion of **perceptions.** For example, something as seemingly measurable as "support for ISAF" must manifest itself ultimately in behavioral terms. How can we possibly know there is support for our troops if we were not observing specific types (or absence) of behaviors? It would be meager satisfaction if opinion polls indicated that support for ISAF was buoyant, and yet there was no evidence of that actual support on the ground.

THE MISPLACED REASSURANCE
OF ADVERTISEMENTS

In peaceful western societies, attitudinal communication, which is the basis for most commercial advertising and marketing, is largely used to differentiate between competing product brands. One brand of toothpaste, for example, is not significantly different to another, but if you associate to it through an attitudinal marketing campaign, certain "desirable" qualities or characteristics (for example, extra whitening capability, pleasant breath qualities, etc.), you effectively differentiate it from your competitors in the eyes of the consumer who is now more likely to purchase your brand. As a consumer walking into a supermarket, you will be confronted by an array of different toothpastes, and your decision to purchase may well be swayed by an advertisement you have seen for a particular brand. However, it is important to remember that the consumer, by their presence in the toothpaste aisle of the supermarket, has already made a decision in their mind to make a purchase; their behavior has already been set. Indeed, that behavior would have been pre-determined by their upbringing (always clean your teeth before bed), their education (not cleaning your teeth will cause you painful medical problems), and other social or cultural factors (for example, guys with bad breath don't get girls!). All the advertiser has to do is switch the consumer's behavior from one brand to another — the key is that the consumer was already going to buy toothpaste. But, as will be shown, this is not the situation in which populations in crisis and conflict situations find themselves.

There is much dispute among psychologists over what attitudes **are**, although what they **are not** is often easier to understand: they are not values or beliefs, and not really opinions, which are often terms used interchangeably with attitudes. In practical terms, this means that attitudes are very difficult, in fact all but impossible, to measure accurately as they are influenced by so many other compounding variables. Surveys that ask if an individual is: "slightly happier, much happier or considerably happier" with a particular issue are popular, but of limited validity, since it is almost impossible to delineate such trends across sample groups. This will be examined again in the context of MOEs for IO campaigns. But perhaps the single biggest problem with the use of attitudes is the now significant body of scientific evidence that indicates they bear so little relation to behavior and ultimately, as already asserted, in conflict-ridden societies it is undesirable **behavior** that the military must mitigate. There are numerous studies that show this to be the case.[31] Because the West is a heavily consumer-based society, advertisements and marketing are accepted as an everyday part of daily life. Indeed, it was this very issue that prompted former U.S. Ambassador Richard Holbrooke's comment, "How can a man in a cave out-communicate the world's leading communications society?"[32] in reaction to Bin Laden, al-Qaeda, and the Taliban's insistent and seemingly compelling rhetoric. Although superficially there would appear to be two competing brands in Afghanistan, the Taliban and the Afghan government, Afghanistan is not a peaceful western democracy, with potential "consumers" waiting to make a choice.

While the Government of the Islamic Republic of Afghanistan (GIRoA) and ISAF may bring reconstruction projects, it might also be argued that they also bring corruption and a return of the hated warlords. Where the Taliban may have mistreated women and banned music, enjoyment, fun, and all those attributes that make life complete, it might also be argued that they bring efficient and quick justice, that they are not "foreigners" and, perhaps most importantly, are seen to be less corrupt than GIRoA. Afghans, unlike U.S. consumers, are not compliant audiences waiting to be steered in a particular direction like the metaphorical toothpaste consumer, nor do NATO PsyOps necessarily reflect what is actually happening on the ground. The example of ISAF roadside billboards illustrates this point. The billboard in Figure 6 extols the virtue and loyalty of the Afghan National Security Forces and is clearly designed to inspire confidence among those who see it. This would be valid in a compliant society, one in which the rule of law is the norm. Yet in a society where corruption is endemic, where successful passage through a checkpoint will almost certainly require the giving of some money, such attitudinal communication does not stack up against the pragmatic reality of life on the ground.

Figure 6. Bill Board ANSF.

For the nonsocial scientist, a simple consideration of many circumstances in our own lives will lead us to the same conclusions. An illustrative example is that for many years governments sought to persuade drivers of the positive benefits of wearing a seat belt when in the car through various attitudinal and informational advertisements which highlight the death and injury rates for car passengers not wearing seat belts. Yet these largely failed, and it took compulsory enforcement (punishable by a fine) through legislation to make the wearing of seat belts an accepted and unconscious activity. Today, particularly if you are North European, it is almost guaranteed that drivers put on a seat belt as an unconscious act as soon as they get into a car and will point out, often disapprovingly, if they see someone not wearing one.

This example reinforces Hutchinson and Warren's 2010 conclusions on "Influence Operations and Behavioural Change"[33] as noted earlier, while attitude is a poor precursor to behavior, behavior is actually a very strong precursor to attitude. Or in other words, if you change behavior, even in noncomplaint audiences, there is a good chance that, with time, their attitude will follow suit—as in the example of the seatbelt. Because the West is so attuned to and accepting of attitudinal communication that it takes a real leap of faith to convince military commanders that advertisements and marketing will not achieve the operational effect they seek. But new developments in behavioral communication, facilitated through social science and behavioral economic research, provide a new avenue that deserves much greater senior attention and which may actually dismiss advertising and marketing as MISO concepts from the battlefield.

This will run counter to many previous high profile studies. In 2007, Todd Helmus, Christopher Paul, and Russell Glenn produced *Enlisting Madison Avenue: The Marketing Approach to Earning Popular Support in Theaters of Operation*.[34] This report declared that: "Business marketing practices provide a useful framework for improving US military efforts to shape attitudes and behaviors of local populations." In particular, the paper declared that attention should be paid to "branding, customer satisfaction, and segmentation of audiences." The segmentation of audiences is a standard marketing technique that looks to sub-divide a specific sector of known consumers—perhaps based on demographics or income or postal address—in the hope that the characteristics of this segmented group will be susceptible to a specific marketing campaign. However this is very much a "push" activity and the "group" is actually an artificial construct that exists only on the marketer's spreadsheet. In military operations, the groups are real, bonded by a myriad of factors outside our control. It would be wonderful if, for example, the U.S. IO job could be done by targeting only the affluent, or the middle-aged, or women in a specific area. But in theaters of operations, the U.S. and its allies do not have the luxury of choosing groups, the United States has to deal with groups that have self-selected — for example, the Mhadi army in southern Iraq or the Haqqani network in Afghanistan.

The job for the IO community is to understand the actual group as it exists, not invent a new one, and to decode the circumstances under which that group may be motivated to exhibit (or not) a specific behavior. This is the process of TAA, and it is very different from the market segmentation used in advertising. Commercial marketing and advertising methods are designed to increase the hit rate of customers in a target group. A conversion rate of 10 percent (i.e., 1 in 10 buying a different brand of car or toothpaste) would be considered outstanding and for a large company may well prove highly profitable. But in military operations achieving a 10 percent change in the behavior of, say, an insurgent group or a hostile community is highly unlikely to be game changing in the context of the wider conflict.

Another factor that derives from advertising being a very well-understood and accepted concept in the very heavily commercialized western world is that there exists an arguable unwritten contract between marketer and potential customer. For example, some of the most popular TV shows have the longest advertising segments. Consumers watch these programs with an implicit acceptance of the advertisements. They are watched in the full knowledge that companies are trying to persuade the consumer to buy more of their products. But this contract does not translate to the battlefield. Indeed, in *Positioning: The Battle for your Mind*[35] — one of the most successful marketing books of all time — the authors clearly make the point that marketing cannot change the way that people think. As the Associate Director of the Pew Global Attitudes Project recently wrote:

> negative views of America remain stubbornly persistent in key Muslim countries. Much of this animosity is due to continuing concerns about U.S. power and widespread opposition to major elements of American foreign policy."[36]

In short, many Muslims, moderate or otherwise, believe very strongly and implicitly that the United States is at war with Islam.

That they do is largely the result of the creation of a single narrative, a version of history that emphasizes Islam's struggle against victimization. It is highly selective and the extent to which it is accepted by its audience — like any communication — depends largely upon their circumstance, in particular their education and their existing view of the world. However, it is undeniably compelling, and it is around this that al-Qaeda and its associates build the legitimacy of their actions. The narrative is based on an interpretation of both historical events and theological references, but at its heart is the fact that Islam is the last revelation of God — for it post-dated Christ by over 1,400 years. Since it is the last revelation, so the narrative goes, it must therefore be the final and absolute word of God, and to deviate from it is heretical. The narrative's authors have long memories. They note, for example, that Pope Urban II (1042-99) launched the crusades in 1095, besieging and slaughtering the population of Jerusalem, which remained captive until Sala-ad

Din's triumphal return in 1187.[37] The colonial period is portrayed as the enslavement of Muslim people by Western oppressors—specifically the UK—while the discovery of oil in 1932 is portrayed as Western exploitation—specifically by the United States—as is the dismantlement of the Ottoman Empire—the last Caliphate. The Sykes-Picot agreement, the Balfour declaration, the Suez crisis—all are seen not as discrete moments in history, but as a continuum of a premeditated war against Islam. Wrapped around the narrative is the claim that Christianity and Judaism seek to destroy Islam, for which selective interpretations of Koranic verses help strengthen the argument. The West, so the narrative runs, proclaims values of fairness, justice, democracy, and equality, and it undermines them whenever Muslims aspire to the selfsame values. Hamas, for example, is democratically elected in the Gaza strip, and yet the West refuses to recognize it and responds with sanctions against the Palestinian people; the West supports Arab regimes in Saudi Arabia, Kuwait, Bahrain, Jordan, *et al.*, where free speech is denied, where elections are rigged, and where torture is a natural consequence of speaking out. The West facilitated the creation of an illegal state, one brought into being by means of so-called Zionist terrorism—Israel—yet refuses to sanction the creation of the state of Palestine. The European Union opens its doors to Greeks but refuses Muslim Turks. In the Former Republic of Yugoslavia, Christian Croatia is allowed by the West to break away, but when Muslim Bosnia does so, it is savagely attacked by Serbia. Refusing to allow armaments to enter Bosnia, the West stands by while Muslims are ethnically cleansed by Christians. In Iraq, the West uses white phosphorous; in Abu Ghraib and Guatanamo, it systematically abuses human rights; Britain publishes Salman Rushdie's book, *The Satanic Verses*; Denmark publishes cartoons of the Prophet Mohamed; and Belgium bans the veil — all vilify Islam, all with the supposed justification of the presumption of free speech. These are the modern crusades, and even the 43rd U.S. President has admitted as much.

On February 20, 1952, one of the "fathers" of Britain's Political Warfare Executive, Richard Crossman, gave an address to the Royal United Services Institute, London, on Psychological Warfare in World War II. In a long and detailed explanation of how his organization had helped defeat the Nazis, he observed:

> The advertiser believed that somehow you could get people to surrender by giving them sales talk. He used to say, "Do you suffer from National Socialism? — Buy British Democracy" on the same lines as "Do you suffer from Body Odor — Buy deodorant." That sort of thing does not work; it is too obvious . . . the usual advertising methods are not efficacious.[38]

Martin F. Herz was chief Leaflet writer for the PsyOps division in SHAEF during World War II. In the 1949 Autumn edition of *The Public Opinion Quarterly*, he wrote:

> The dispersion of themes in some of our combat propaganda may have been caused in part by the advertising and journalism background of many of our propagandists. Combat propaganda and other propaganda addressed to enemy populations in wartime posed quite different problems than domestic advertising![39]

In marketing, the desired behavior is fairly uniform, and quite predictable: "Buy our product." The whole campaign, from planning to research to execution, wraps linearly around the trajectory of selling a product. Yet, this does not map to the sorts of behaviors we seek to influence in conflict areas such as Afghanistan, or indeed the wider Muslim world, where negative views are so very widely entrenched. Commercial marketing is not the kind of discipline that is equipped to deal with behavioral outcomes or scenarios that are more complex or require more nuanced definitions. It is this author's view that marketing principles are simply not effective enough to drive U.S. military capabilities and development; and that the end of that road will only be failure. Further, it is this author's view that only a scientific approach will do. This approach must be based on the sciences pertaining to human behavior, in all its myriad manifestations and with all its bewildering complexities, and not the limited perspective of consumer behavior, or the misguided assumptions of attitudinal psychology.

Unfortunately, the special knowledge necessary to do this is neither held in the U.S. military community, nor for that matter in almost all of the contractors for which the U.S. Government has priming arrangements. The U.S. contractual system is bewildering, and while it understandably seeks to place U.S. governmental business with U.S. companies, there is a real issue when customers — U.S. military commands — are locked into contractual arrangements with companies that simply do not have the necessary expertise to undertake the desired tasks. This has been most recently demonstrated by a specialist UK company that was contacted by a combatant command (CCMD) for deep specialist TAA services. Or rather they would have been had the CCMD not been locked into a binding arrangement with a huge U.S. service provider that, sensing revenue, refused to subcontract the work, claiming they could undertake it themselves. With no demonstrable background in TAA provision, the CCMD rather wisely refused to let them have the business. In the face of such bureaucratic constraints, the CCMD chose not to let the contract at all and the work, an operational assessment of a high priority audience, was not undertaken.

MEASURES OF EFFECT

Former U.S. Ambassador to Afghanistan and now trustee of the Asia Foundation, Karl Eikenberry, wrote in *The Financial Times*[40] in late 2012 that "There is yet hope for Afghanistan," and that a recent Asia Foundation Poll proved it. He wrote:

> . . . 52 per cent of the people believe it is moving in the right direction; 93 per cent have great or fair confidence in their armed forces; 89 per cent give the government good marks for the provision of education; 72 per cent say their national legislature is addressing the problems of ordinary citizens; and 50 per cent assert their financial wellbeing has improved over the past 12 months? Not the US, Singapore, or Brazil. Answer: Afghanistan.

Such pronouncements rely on polling. Consider a typical polling question:

Q. Do you think the security situation around your home is:
> A. A lot worse than last year.
> B. Worse than last year?
> C. The same as last year?
> D. Better than last year?
> E. A lot better than last year?

Now what is the precise difference between answers A and B; or D and E? By what authoritative comparators can a respondent judge if the security situation today is the same as a year ago? What counts as "a lot" to one respondent may not even register with another respondent, even if they come from the same family. Each person's perception of events is different and will be based upon individual experiences and influences. This type of polling question lacks any kind of scientific precision and is also highly subjective to each respondent, and each respondent's views are highly temporal. In 2010, the Asia Foundation published a poll result that claimed 84 percent of respondents agreed that the ANP was "honest and fair." This seems a rather high figure for a nation-state in transition from civil war. One way of, perhaps, benchmarking it is to compare it with other nations, for example the United States and the UK. In 2011, the UK's customer satisfaction with local police services was rated as 71 percent[41] – a lower figure than that for the ANP. Does 71 percent seem a fair representation of British support for the police? The truth is that it is almost impossible to tell: actual behavior is perhaps the only useful indicator. For example, to someone living in a small(ish) village with a very low crime rate and just a couple of very friendly community police officers, that satisfaction rating might seem unduly low. Yet, for a poorly educated and low income young black man in a depressed inner city area, that figure might seem far too high. Indeed, a recent report posited that hatred of the British police was a primary cause of the London riots of August 2011.[42] How, then, can a national survey, with so many different polarized views, give a fair indication of the genuine levels of support, or lack of support for the police in the UK or, for that matter, the Afghan Security Forces? The U.S. Department of Justice has apparently recognized this problem, and in their own report into U.S. citizens' satisfaction with their police departments, highlighted:

> Different individuals respond differently to quality-of-life surveys even though they are exposed to similar neighborhood conditions. Moreover, persons from the same neighborhood report different levels of satisfaction with Police—these inconsistencies limit the relevance of . . . [these surveys].[43]

All of this raises the question of why, if these types of survey are not appropriate for U.S. police forces and so plainly at odds with the reality of UK policing, are they considered suitable for guiding major policy decisions about Afghanistan? What is particularly interesting is that, while in 2010 the Asia Foundation was busy polling, another, more detailed qualitative data gathering operation was being conducted in Maiwand Province by the British company, SCL. SCL is almost unique in the international contractor community in that it has a dedicated, and funded, behavioral research arm located in the prestigious home of British science and research, The Royal Institute, London. The results of their survey were quite different and indicated widespread disillusionment with, low confidence in, and fear of the ANP.

What is the acid test for polling? This author would suggest that poll results must agree with anecdotal experiences and reports derived from being out on the ground in Afghanistan talking to people. Since the Asia Foundation poll does not agree with personal experience on the ground nor does it stand up to a simple benchmarking exercise, it perhaps should be treated with skepticism. Polls, however well they are produced, cannot be more than a comforting hand rail for policymakers and cannot be substitutes for more empirically based qualitative research.

The 2012 RAND report on U.S. IO identified the absence of robust and empirical MOE as one of its key findings. Without MOE, it is almost impossible to draw any sensible conclusions on the success, or otherwise, of IO campaigns. The fact that Congress was unable to be persuaded that its past expenditure on U.S. IO had been worthwhile is indicative itself that the programs provided by contractors lacked empirically derived TAA which, in turn, means they lacked academic rigor. It should also be obvious that MOE can only be applied to behaviors. Either a behavior exists, or it does not. It may reduce or increase, but it is measurable. If the campaign is to grow less poppy, you can visibly see if that campaign has been successful from the air. If the campaign is to encourage greater use of, for example, Highway 611 (the major north-south route that goes from Lashkar Gah to Sangin in Helmand, Afghanistan) by private cars (thus fostering a feeling of security), you can easily measure road usage with a few strategically placed motion sensors. You could even measure accurately the numbers of calls to a hotline that led to successful arrests or locating IEDs.

Only through TAA baselining can MOE be derived. The absence of a TAA derived baseline is an immediate indicator to intelligent customers that the proposed program is unlikely to work. If any thought is given to MOE, then it is regularly in the context of measures of performance (MOP) or measures of activity (MOA). For example, the MOA associated with an airborne leaflet drop is that the necessary aircraft and equipment were serviceable and available to make a certain number of predetermined sorties. The MOP is that a specific number of leaflets or other products were dropped. The MOE, however, is the specific action(s) that the leaflets engendered in the audiences that they targeted.

Conversely, attitudinal campaigns are not measurable in any meaningful manner. This is why surveys and polling have blossomed so fully during the wars in Iraq and Afghanistan[44]—and, we would contend, with such disastrous results. The focus has been on attitudes, and surveys and polling are a logical if imperfect way to measure whether attitudes have changed.

The key to successful MOE is two-fold. First, activity has to be properly base-lined. It is no good attempting measure behaviors, or for that matter attitude, after the IO/PSYOPS intervention if there is no record of what the behavior or attitude was prior to it. There are several issues involved here.

a. **Establishing behavioral indicators.** From the outset, it is necessary to identify appropriate behavioral indicators by which to measure change. This requires an in-depth understanding of the target group and their behavioral patterns, and a sufficiently rich awareness of which behaviors are most indicative of change. It is hard to do this in the beginning and actually must be based on high quality TAA of the prospective audience(s) to narrow down the possibilities. Often, several iterations may be needed to get this right.

b. **Causality versus causation.** The real devil in all this is how to unravel the competing effects of factors that **cause** the behavior change and those that are merely **correlated** with change. A well-worn but classic example is that ice-cream sales increase in line with the numbers of drownings. This does not imply, though, that one caused the other. It is more likely that a third factor, hot weather, underlies both increases. How can we distinguish whether retention in the ANA has improved due to our behavioral campaign, or because more insurgents have infiltrated the ranks and wish to build up numbers for attacks from within? It is difficult to perform analyses of this kind, but, if approached scientifically, it is possible. Prominent U.S. social psychologist Timothy Wilson has criticized the Drug, Abuse, Resistance & Education (D.A.R.E) anti-drug program which is used by 70 percent of American schools, and yet, until recently, had never been tested. He explained on "The Edge" social science website:

> If there's one thing social psychologists do know how to do, it's how to do experiments and how to test whether an intervention is working, and with good control groups and statistical analyses, seeing whether something works or not. Yet, a lot of the current programs in a wide variety of areas have never been vetted in that way, and are just based on common sense.[45]

The testing Wilson referred to revealed a shocking result: the program did not work. In fact, Wilson believed the program could even have increased drug abuse among the target population. MOE needs to be based on rigorous scientific testing, not on weak *post hoc* or supplementary measures.

    c. **Changes in audience.** Part of fulfilling the criteria above can be achieved by recognizing that there are multiple stages of change (one influential behavior model by Prochaska and DeClemete[46] is called the "stages of change" model), and that these can and should be measured. By doing so, we can get a more accurate description of how change is occurring and to what extent it relates to military actions. Between basic behavioral indicators and the kinds of large-scale behavior changes that campaigns seek to measure, many changes occur at the audience level that are more subtle, yet highly predictive of behavioral outcomes. These will include attitudes, intentions, motivational dispositions, and perceptions, and they need to be measured, too; not as an end in themselves, but as ways of gauging intermediate changes in target groups.

MOE is not just vital to behaviorally based projects (and almost impossible in attitudinally based products), but it is also vital for one higher strategic reason. Without robust and proven MOE, savvy politicians—with many deserving and competing demands upon scarcer fiscal resources—rightly find it hard to see or demonstrate return on investment. In the U.S. IO program thus far, they have not seen this at all. As the U.S. Committee on Appropriations reported in 2010:

> The Committee believes that the Department of Defense, and the Combatant Commands which drive the demand for information operations, need to reevaluate IO requirements in the context of the roles and missions of the United States Military along with consideration for the inherent capabilities of the military and the funding available to meet these requirements. In support of this evaluation, the Committee has determined that many of the ongoing IO activities for which fiscal year 2010 funding is requested should be terminated immediately.[47]

Achieving More for Less.

In 2007 the UK Defence Academy produced a limited-distribution briefing paper entitled *The Realities of Defense Economics*. In a paragraph entitled "The

Problem of the Defense Budget," it made the following observations:

> For 300 years, during peacetime, the English / UK Defence Budget has been remarkably consistent at between 2-5% of GDP [gross domestic product]. At 2-3% GDP—without the running costs of current operations, we cannot sustain the capability to conduct the full spectrum of military operations that we have in the past. To do that, we would need 4-5% GDP. Even to maintain our current reduced capabilities and associated minimal structures, Defence needs more money than it is getting. Conclusion: Either we need a serious increase in the Defence Budget or we need to introduce drastic changes in the way we do things. (And most likely, we need a combination of the two). "Drastic Change" could be in:
> - how we procure equipment, what we buy, how we make it, etc.;
> - personnel policies—how we manage careers, man our units, ships, etc.;
> - how we structure and use reserves;
> - whether we are content to have Armed Forces with only "niche capabilities";
> - how we develop non-military ways of taking on and defeating an opponent.

It is the last bullet that is of most interest to this discussion. To see the most dramatic advances in thinking on "using nonmilitary ways of taking on and defeating an opponent," we should look to the aspirations to nonmilitary strategic effect of several countries.

China.

The People's Republic of China (PRC) perceives future warfare evolving into a battle for full spectrum dominance—Military, Political, Economic, and

Diplomatic. In each of these, the PRC recognizes that influence (as a noun) is absolutely central, and accordingly has proactively grown what it refers to as its three warfares (*san zhong zhanfa*) concept.[48] These are the principal enablers (what this monograph defined earlier as the verbs of influence) which are aimed at preconditioning key areas of competition in its favor through mastery of psychological warfare, media warfare, and legal warfare. As the U.S. DoD's annual report to Congress 2011 noted:

> In 2003, the CCP Central Committee and the CMC endorsed the three warfare concept, reflecting China's recognition that as a global actor, it will benefit from learning to effectively utilize the tools of public opinion, messaging, and **influence** [author's highlighting]. China likely hopes to employ these three concepts in unison, particularly during the early stages of a crisis, as they have a tendency to bolster one another.[49]

In their January 2012 report, *China's Three Warfares*, Delex Consulting noted that the Chinese are aiming for a "high degree of precision in targeting critical nodes to achieve non-linear effects."[50] As part of China's developing asymmetric strategy, the People's Liberation Army (PLA) has developed capabilities, referred to as "Assassin's Mace" (*sha shou jian*) programs, which have been designed to give technologically inferior military advantages over technologically superior adversaries, and thus change the direction of a conflict. Since the late 1990s, the term has appeared more frequently in Chinese military publications and journals, particularly in the context of any potential conflict with the United States over the issue of, for example, Taiwanese sovereignty.[51]

There is insufficient English language literature in open sources to determine what does or does not constitute "assassin's mace"; however, in a country that spawned Sun Tzu and his seminal proclamation that: "The supreme art of war is to subdue the enemy without fighting," it would seem likely that ideas of applied behavioral change, and in particular the TAA that underpins it, if not already part of the Chinese military lexicon, will be soon. Timothy Thomas of the U.S. Foreign Military Studies Office (FMSO) notes in his book, *Dragon Bytes*, that:

> In 'The Doctrine of Psychological Operations in Ancient China,' Wu Juncang and Zhang Qiancheng note that China's history of psychological operations goes back more than four thousand years [and] . . . those early psychological experiences culminated in Sun Tzu's Art of War, which describes the main objective of war as defeating the enemy without having to fight; the main essence of war as attacking the enemy's strategy; the main principle of war as contending for control of hearts, minds and morale; and the main idea of war as focusing on the enemy commander's decision-making skills and personal traits.[52]

How does the United States and its allies, particularly those around the Pacific rim, deal with the challenges of a strident Chinese government exercising territorial claims and casting ambitions for future resources? It could, of course, demonstrate military capability through military exercises. This would be a perfectly legitimate response but one which the Chinese would have already considered and modeled for response options. The United States may choose to escalate exercising to force, or indeed it may happen by accident; neither is a palatable contingency. It could embark upon an attitudinal based IO program, much as has been the practice in recent years, although we would suggest that from the evidence presented earlier, it really should not. It has certainly already embarked upon diplomatic and economic activities, and we would suggest both will be carefully studied and publicly mitigated by China.

Current thinking and past best practice is all very predictable by the Chinese who have a track record of watching, learning, and adapting. As the DoD report has noted, the Chinese Armed Forces may not have the military sophistication of the United States yet, but it is growing. It seems likely that they are supplementing hard kinetic capability with soft IO capability. While the Chinese aircraft carrier fleet remains physically embryonic, it is globally emblematic:

> The development of aircraft carriers is an important part of China's national defense modernization, in particular its naval forces, and this aircraft carrier is an essential stepping stone toward its own more advanced aircraft carriers in the future.[53]

Of course, it is likely to take years before China is able to undertake "carrier diplomacy"[54] but, during that period, clumsy carrier-related rhetoric and deployment may well exacerbate tensions; and in the absence of hard physical military power, why would the Chinese not embark upon alternative means of achieving effect? One has to look at other areas of innovation to see that the Chinese are neither risk adverse nor cash strapped. Perhaps what is most interesting from the 2006 Chinese experiment to use ground based lasers to blind U.S. reconnaissance satellites is the comment of Director of the National Office of Reconnaissance Donald Kerr: "It makes us think."[55] There is plenty to think about. For example, in *Unrestricted Warfare*,[56] a book published in China in February 1999 which proposes tactics for China to compensate for their military inferiority vis-à-vis the United States, the authors state that it may become "necessary to use special means to wage psychological war aimed at soldiers' families far back in the rear area."

China's willingness to engage in sensitive issues in nonconventional military ways is exemplified by the "Twitter War" that erupted in March 2012 over the issue of Tibet.[57] This saw bots flooding discussions with the hashtags, #Tibet and #Freetibet, threatening Tibetan activists and condemning those who had died through self-immolation. Although this was perhaps the first Chinese major hostile IO campaign to receive serious attention overseas, it followed a series of similar programs over recent years tied to specific economic and security objectives.[58] Indeed, the beginning of 2013 saw media reporting of a brigade, possibly called *waumao* and numbering as many as 60,000 people, who are paid 75 U.S. cents per Tweet by the ruling Chinese regime to say positive things about the Communist Party on the Chinese equivalent of Twitter, *Weibo*.[59] As one commentator suggested, China sees *Weibo* as the ultimate arena for Chinese public opinion.

Russia.

China is by no means the only country to be actively engaging in focused IO — Russia, too, has tested their utility. According to research undertaken by the U.S. FMSO, Russia has:

two aspects to its IO theory: information-technical and information psychological. Not only are these different from the US's "assigned and supporting capabilities and activities," but Russia also views Information Superiority differently. Russian theorists place as much emphasis on "disorganizing" the enemy as they do toward achieving information superiority. In fact, they believe the former produces the latter.[60]

In the years following the overthrow of the Tsar of Russia, Vladimir Lenin's secret services — the *Cheka* — adopted an idea that the Soviets were later to embrace — *Maskirovka*. This is a term that has no direct equivalent in the West, but it simultaneously encompasses the arts of:

> concealment, the use of dummies and decoys, disinformation and even the execution of complex demonstration maneuvers. Indeed anything capable of . . . weakening the enemy.[61]

Indeed, conscious that the Union of Soviet Socialist Republics (USSR) would struggle to match the pace of technological investment of the United States, the Soviets actively sought alternatives to hard power, and, by the late 1950s, scientists began studying physical and social regulatory systems. Using newly developed computer technology, scientists were directed to consider military decisionmaking. In doing so, they created a modeling system comprised of three subsystems: a model to simulate one's own decisions, a model to simulate the adversary's systems, and a model to actually make decisions. The model's inventor, Vladimir Lefebvre, concluded that this model could be used to influence an adversary into making decisions that were favorable to the Soviet Union. Lefebvre argued that:

> In making his decisions, the adversary uses information about the area of conflict, about his own troops and ours, about their ability to fight, etc. We can influence his channels of information and send messages that shift the flow of information in a way favorable to us.[62]

In essence, Lefebvre was suggesting that if the Soviet Union could get inside the decisionmaking process of the adversary and understand that process, it could provide the adversary with information and conditions which might lead it to make a predetermined decision. According to Lebvfre, rather than looking at conflict as an interaction between two military forces, conflict should be considered as being between the decisionmaking processes of the two opponents, where each adversary bases his decisions on a model of both himself and his adversary — i.e., a reflective interaction between the two. K. V. Tarakanov explains the process thus:

> Reflexive control is understood as the process of one of the sides giving reasons to the enemy from which he can logically infer his own decision, pre-determined by the first side . . . reflexive control should be understood as the reflection by the opposed sides in the thoughts of their discussions with each other.[63]

Or, from more contemporary literature:

> Reflexive control is defined as a means of conveying to a partner or an opponent specially prepared information to incline him to voluntarily make the predeter-

mined decision desired by the initiator of the action. Even though the theory was developed long ago in Russia, it is still undergoing further refinement. Recent proof of this is the development in February 2001, of a new Russian journal known as Reflexive Processes and Control. The journal is not simply the product of a group of scientists but, as the editorial council suggests, the product of some of Russia's leading national security institutes, and boasts a few foreign members as well.[64]

Russian theorist S. A. Komov offered a series of theoretical examples of the deployment of reflexive control:

- Distraction—during preparatory stages of combat operations, creating a real or imaginary threat against one of the most vital enemy places such as flanks and rear, forcing him to reevaluate his decisions to operate on this or that axis.
- Overload—often manifested by sending the enemy a large amount of conflicting information.
- Paralysis—creating the belief of a specific threat to a vital interest or weak spot.
- Suggestion—offer information that affects the enemy legally, morally, ideologically, or in other areas.[65]

Of course, military sophistication and preparedness is not necessarily something that we associate with contemporary Russia. Since the end of the Cold War, imagery of decrepit Russian warships driven ashore on remote peninsulas, an unpaid conscript army, and low morale seem to have characterized public coverage of the former Soviet "bear." Yet, during the period of underfunding of physical and kinetic capability,

Russia continued to develop advanced theoretical and strategic concepts such as reflexive control. FMSO believes they do so because "Russians believe that a single global 'information space' is emerging, which could allow a country to exploit this space and alter the global balance of power,"[66] continuing that "Russian security specialists believe that no issue is more important or more fraught with uncertainty than the current and future information environment."[67]

FMSO suggests a number of reasons why this is so. First, it notes that people have unprecedented access to information, which allows citizens and decision-makers alike a variety of choices. This comes at a time when many Russians are:

> still searching for an ideology or set of principles in which they can find the values and purposes for their very existence. Under such conditions, the mass media, especially television and the press, play a much more important role than ever before.[68]

Second, Russians perceive that information itself has developed into a very important type of national or strategic resource. The "informatization" of society influences financial markets, business practices, and even the capabilities of military weapons. FMSO states that:

> Russians believe that countries that possess 'information superiority' may be more inclined than before to employ military force. Military objectives may seem more attainable without significant loss of life and with no apparent ecological risk to such countries. Many Russians believe that the recent NATO intervention in Kosovo was based on the dictate of information superiority, thereby virtually guaranteeing a NATO victory.[69]

Third, Russians realize that few legal restraints exist that can regulate information interventions or even attacks. This factor also encourages the growth of concepts such as cyber terrorism, specifically the use by terrorists of information means to penetrate or destroy information security systems of banks, military institutions, or vital societal assets (power stations and other infrastructure facilities and systems). As Professor of Political Science Stephen Cimbala notes:

> Russia's military is aware of US . . . superiority in advanced technological conventional warfare. Therefore Russian security experts have studied the importance of indirect approaches to offsetting US Superiority, including asymmetrical information strategies.[70]

Most recently this has manifested itself as soft force—the term coined by Moscow State University lecturer Andrey Pronin which will present the United States with an "ideological challenge," repeating, Pronin argues, the success of the USSR which was able to split the West and find itself numerous allies.[71]

These Russian ideas are of direct relevance to the 21st century, and in particular to U.S. IO programs. Lieutenant Colonel (Retired) Charles Blandy served as a leading expert at the British precursor of FMSO, the UK Defence Academy's Conflict Studies Research Centre (CSRC). Blandy believes that he can see evidence of reflexive control in the lead-up to Russia's incursion into Georgia in 2008. Blandy writes that:

> the Soviet and Russian general staffs, over a long period of time, have studied the application of reflexive control theory . . . in order to influence and control an enemy's decision making process.[72]

Blandy believes that Georgian President Mikheil Saakashvili's character and personality made him ripe for a reflexive control operation. Saakashvili was:

> hot headed, often rash in his decisions and intemperate. In my view the Russians knew how to raise the political pressure on him and also what he would do when the pressure became unbearable.[73]

That pressure had been gradually, and according to Blandy deliberately, raised by Russia's intense international political bullying over the issue of the semiautonomous Republics of South Ossetia and Abkhazia for some years. However it was, in Blandy's view, intensified by the deployment of Russian troops in the spring of 2008 to Abkhazia—for President Saakashvili this was a well signposted step too far. Blandy notes, in particular, the publication in the Russian military newspaper, *Krasnaya Zvezda*, of a detailed psychological profile of Saakashvili, indicative, in Blandy's view, of the studies and assessments that would have formed a useful template for shaping the Georgian President's decisions.[74]

The Norwegian Ministry of Defence would also appear to agree. In a 2010 briefing to NATO, they concluded that the Russian IO Campaign was focused on four strategic objectives: (1) discredit and criminalize Georgian operations as genocide; (2) undermine the credibility of President Saakashvili; (3) legitimize its own invasion of South Ossetia; and (4) use CNO to cut Georgian communications at the critical early stages of the campaign. The desired end state, according to the Norwegians, was twofold: to prevent NATO intervention and support for Georgia, and to solidify internal domestic Russian support.[75]

Georgia has not been the only example of a growing Russian willingness to engage in overt IO at a pre-conflict stage. The cyber attacks on Estonia are well documented but less so is the apparent incessant Russian IO focus on Estonia's Baltic neighbors, Lithuania and Latvia. At a NATO PsyOps Conference held in Vilnius, Lithuania, in the fall of 2012, Lithuanian and Latvian IO officers provided the conference with a detailed presentation on how, in their view, Russia was proactively seeking to discredit the idea of Lithuanian (and Latvian) national identity. This, they demonstrated, was being undertaken by a series of concerted and organized IO activities, notably in the cultural, television, sporting, and performing domains. They also highlighted how Lithuania's Special Forces, Artivas, and their operations in Afghanistan had become the subject of concerted public exposure.

TAA and Strategic Deterrence.

Arguably one of the biggest historical weaknesses in U.S. strategy has been the absence of a proper "Understand" capability. In the 1970s, military theorist and former U.S. Air Force officer John Boyd devised a concept that is still taught in western defense academies today—the OODA (Observe, Orient, Decide, and Act) loop. Yet, it might be argued that the U.S. standing capacity to orient in advance of future crises has repeatedly been found wanting. This has been compounded by an over-reliance on the views of national intelligence collection agencies, who are, in essence, short-term collectors rather than long-term trend analysts. One might cite the examples of the Yom Kippur War, the Iranian Revolution, the Soviet invasion of Afghanistan, the collapse of the Soviet Union, the fall of the Berlin Wall, India's 1998 nuclear tests, the 9/11 attacks, and the Arab Spring, none of which were predicted by the United States. In effect, this, then, leads to something more resembling an "ODA" loop: Observe that something in the world has gone wrong; Decide that some form of reactive response is required; and then Act, responding later to whatever consequences may follow.

The United States is by no means alone in falling into this trap of taking precipitate action without orienting for second- and third-order consequences. Many other states have done the same, but history shows surprisingly few examples of states that successfully anchored their foreign policy on preemptive orientation (Understanding). Yet, TAA is the perfect vehicle to grow this preemptive understanding. Imagine a mechanism where TAA is being conducted continuously on the top 10 or so countries of interest to the United States, with the key groups, formed or emerging, being studied, their motivations being mapped. This is not conventional intelligence gathering, this is using proven and behavioral science techniques to predict what groups might rise to preeminence, given certain conditions and motivators and what behaviors those groups might exhibit. This knowledge is invaluable in its own right—but when it is used to model likely intervention scenarios, it becomes a very specialized tool indeed, one that can genuinely assist in strategic long-term planning as opposed short-term reactive action. We could even term this strategic deterrence because, armed with the necessary motivational understanding and having modeled different influence interventions, the United States and its allies can properly plan for the unexpected, and publicly or privately inform its allies and adversaries accordingly. This model would more than address the comment by Brooks highlighted at the very start of this monograph:

> Strategic communication is a confusing term, but one that has nonetheless come to stand for something complex and important, something that has more to do with strategy than with communications.[76]

TAA and China.

For all the improvements in military thinking with respect to cultural, anthropological, and sociological understanding (and we think here in particular of HTT), a TAA program, with downstream influence intervention, is the work of highly specialized commercial providers not government agencies. TAA is far too complex and must be conducted in-county by organic nationals, with some degree of separation from their U.S. sponsor. This requires a degree of subtlety and agility that may not be possible for governmental agencies. In any event, the protocols for analyzing this data are so complex that they cannot be mirrored any time soon by governmental agencies. The U.S. Government has already been the principal consumer of robust behavioral change programs and as the U.S. Government Accountability Office's report, *US Public Diplomacy – Actions Needed to Improve Strategic Use and Coordination of Research*, noted "the central importance of research in focusing on behaviour change."[77]

This will prove particularly important in understanding China's future ambitions. In 2005, Deputy U.S. Secretary of State Robert Zoellick called on China — as a country that had transformed itself largely as a result of its participation in the international system—to take on a greater leadership role within that system. In Zoellick's words: "As a responsible stakeholder, China would be more than just a member—it would work with us to sustain the international system that has enabled its success."[78] However, as the U.S.-China Economic and Security Review Commission noted in their 2011 report:

> Although China's role and stake in the international system has only increased in the intervening 5 years, there has been little appreciable evidence that they have accepted the Zoellick argument on being a responsible stakeholder.[79]

Indeed, one might suggest that this was always an unrealistic expectation based on a poor TAA of the Chinese position and its ambitions. Why would China, for example, seek to advance an international system established at Bretton Woods in 1944, some 5 years before the PRC in its present form was created, which solidifies the U.S. position of global hegemony? China may well have huge international aid programs; but make no mistake, China's international activities are far from altruistic. Its soft power effort is enormous and seeks to benefit only one recipient in the long run—China. The Three Warfares concept is an example of China's willingness to adapt to a changing environment, not necessarily conform to the status quo. It is presumed that the United States will not wish to engage in overt military conflict with the PRC. Indeed, the United States has been at pains to emphasis that it seeks "neither conflict nor containment"[80] in its Chinese policy. Yet at the same time, the United States may wish to check some of the PRC's more contentious ambitions; not necessarily in a manner visible to the general public. (Indeed, this might be a counterproductive strategy since the need for China to retain "face" may prompt undesirable behavior — for example, the harassment of the USNS *Impeccable* in 2009.)[81] But it must be visible to the Chinese government. It would be strange if a nation that has consistently espoused a holistic view of conflict, from Sun Tzu to the Three Warfares concept, is not already undertaking targeted behavioral influence campaigns of its own. That job is made easier by the huge amount of freely available U.S. and Western doctrine and operational data that a Google search reveals online, the huge Chinese disapora and its connections back to the PRC, the U.S. operations in Afghanistan and Iraq, the openness of the U.S. media, Freedom of Information, and ease of travel and communication. The United States has far fewer of the same advantages when it comes to understanding the workings of the Chinese Communist Party. This is a scenario that is aching for a behavioral approach, but one that needs to start now through the instigation of a robust TAA process of direct and indirect actors.

The Distraction of "Cyber."

This author assesses that there also exists a risk that momentum may be lost because of the rapidly expanding interest in all things "cyber." While the 2007 cyber attacks in Estonia rightly came as a wakeup call to policymakers on both sides of the Atlantic, some observers have suggested that too much time and money is being spent on cyber, perhaps because of its perceived effect in the Arab Spring. Dr. David Betz of London's King's College has written:

Like the shock paddles of a defibrillator on the chest of a heart attack victim the prefix 'cyber' has an electrifying effect on policymakers and strategists wrestling with the complexities of information age security — or more commonly today, 'cybersecurity'. Successfully attaching the term to this or that policy appears to markedly increase its chances of survival. Thus in recent years while public spending has been shrinking (or is expected imminently to shrink) we have seen a bonanza of resources dedicated to countering or mitigating threats to our economic vitality from 'cyber espionage' and 'cyber crime', societal cohesion from 'cyber subversion' and 'cyber terror', and ultimately our material being from 'cyber war'. 'I dare say,' said Deputy Secretary of Defence Ashton B. Carter in March 2012, 'we'd spend a lot more if we could figure out where to spend it . . . the foreign policy community is worried too much about the effect of cyber on the existing distribution of power among states in the international system. It is not worried enough about the ways in which digital connectivity is imbuing a wide range of novel globally networked social movements with a potential strategic significance not seen by non-state actors since 1648.'[82]

Or to put it another way, we are collectively too worried about cyber attacks on our existing societies and their infrastructures by state actors, and not enough on how cyber is facilitating the likely behaviors of disparate nonstate groups; TAA is all about understanding the likely behavior of groups.

Ashton Carter's observation is likely to be of great interest to commercial contractors who will be only too happy to advise on how budgets should be spent. With all the public criticism of IO, it is perhaps unlikely anyone will be championing behavioral issues per se. Indeed, in their response to this author's paper entitled "Why Rand Missed the Point," Rand Corporation's Arturo G. Munoz stated that:

> the most far-reaching, recent innovation in terms of communication and political mobilization is happening on the internet. As we debate recondite issues of attitude and behavior, the world is passing us by.[83]

This is a view given greater airing in RAND's 2013 publication: "Redefining Information Warfare Boundaries For An Army In A Wireless World."[84] Yet this author argues that cyber, like TV, video, and the written word, is but a 21st century facilitator for exchanging already held strong beliefs and behaviors. Certainly cyber facilitates their easy transmission to others, be it a macro or micro scale, locally or internationally, in a way that has not previously been possible. But does watching a video on YouTube guarantee that an individual will sign up for violent jihad? Does subscribing to a particular Twitter feed ensure that the individual will seek out others and plan terrorist attacks? Certainly the Free Syrian Army's regular postings of alleged atrocities in Syria have encouraged some foreign fighters to enter the fray — but not the huge numbers who have seen the videos on YouTube and far fewer than the numbers who joined the anti-Soviet Jihad in 1980s Afghanistan, long before the internet was public knowledge. The point is that the effect of cyber on behavior, and likely behavior, is as indeterminate as the effect of Osama bin Laden's videos. Understanding what motivates specific behavior in particular groups, and how to mitigate that, remains absolutely key.

CONCLUSIONS

To a well-informed, knowledgeable but nevertheless non-U.S. observer, the U.S. SC organization and IO seems to be in a state of some chaos. The public proclamation by George Little that SC was "dead" came as a huge shock, particularly to NATO where considerable effort has gone into persuading, cajoling, and influencing seniors from many different member nations to allocate funding and personnel to the coalition's SC efforts. Worse still has been the dreadful headlines—media, nongovernmental organization (NGO), and in-house—about the failure of U.S. IO in Afghanistan, followed by the various stories about long-standing U.S. contractors such as Leonie Industries[85] and the Rendon Corporation. Unfortunately, it is difficult to argue against the 2012 RAND proposition that:

> if the overall IO mission in Afghanistan is defined as convincing most residents of contested areas to side decisively with the Afghan government and its foreign allies against the Taliban insurgency, this has not been achieved.[86]

Policymakers might therefore be forgiven for considering that, in any review of defense expenditure, SC, and in particular IO, would offer quick and easy cuts to make. It is quite clear that cuts are coming. Since 2001, the U.S. defense budget has nearly doubled from $287 billion to $530 billion,[87] the largest in the world (and bigger than the next 13 nations' defense budgets combined)—and this amount still does not include the ever-growing cost of the wars of choice in Iraq and Afghanistan. *The Washington Post* opined in 2011 that the United States had spent about $718 billion on defense and international security assistance,[88] and approximately \$729 billion in 2012. Professor Christopher Croker of the London School of Economics cites figures showing that the United States has spent more on its current conflicts than it did for all of World War II—and, in his view, with demonstrably less result.[89] At a time of global financial stress, such figures are clearly not sustainable, and as the U.S. Government wavered over sequestration in early 2013, the one point that was abundantly clear was that U.S. defense spending would be reduced, and substantially so. The question was simply where and when the savings be made.

In this monograph, this author has sought to demonstrate that the failings in U.S. SC and IO were not failings of the concept of SC and IO, but of its day-to-day implementation. As demonstrated in Case Study 1, the Afghan wedding dowry program, contractors are unafraid to propose extremely imaginative and self-evidently expensive "solutions" to U.S. problems, particularly when "customers" do not have the necessary experience to understand the nuance of what is being suggested. Case Study 2, the Pakistan TV advertisements, demonstrated how marketing and advertising solutions were being applied to environments where they stood almost no hope of success or where success would be impossible to measure in any empirical manner. These examples represent merely the tip of the iceberg: Over the years, huge amounts of money have been spent on IO programs that are largely anchored in advertising and marketing style communication with little concurrent investment, it would appear, in detailed understanding of audiences and environments. Most of the available doctrinal documentation talks at length about co-ordination, integration, and synchronization of IO across forces and domains. However, there is surprisingly little talk of the need to actually understand the likely motivations for targeted audiences. Anecdotal evidence would suggest that, despite the passage of years, this has remained the Achilles heel of our collective efforts in Afghanistan. Matt Cavanagh, a former advisor to British Prime Minister Tony Blair, recalled the 2006 decision to deploy British forces to Helmand:

> No one inside the British [government] system knew much about the insurgency, the opium trade or the local politics and tribal dynamics—or just as importantly about how these different elements fitted into each other. Planners and policy makers [in 2006] did not know much about the human or even physical geography of Helmand.[90]

In his book, *The Operators*, the late U.S. Journalist Michael Hastings records a meeting of a strategic review panel with senior U.S. briefers:

> In one meeting [Andrew] Exum drills down on the briefers. Who controls the water? Who are the local power brokers? Tell me how they are related to the insurgency. The Intel Officers shrug. The questions 'scare the hell out of them'.[91]

Former commander of ISAF Forces General Stanley McChrystal, in a 2011 speech, told the U.S. Council on Foreign Relations that:

> The U.S. and its NATO allies are only 'a little better than half way' to achieving their military goals, partly due to a frighteningly simplistic understanding of the country.[92]

Without this detailed understanding, I argue that any attempt to influence will be predicated upon luck.

Concurrently, there appears to be an absence of intelligent customers. While staff colleges and military academies prepare military officers and diplomats for career service, experience shows that corporate understanding of even the most basic principles of influence are exceptionally weak. This is not a criticism of individuals, more a statement of fact—careers are made in commanding companies, battalions, brigades and divisions on operations; kinetics prevail. Yet, as the wars of choice in Iraq and Afghanistan have amply demonstrated, kinetic firepower may very well win battles, while the campaigns still flounder. Senior officers are completely familiar with the type of kinetic effects that can be achieved, their risks, operating windows, and likely benefits. Their mastery and application of that knowledge is why they are senior commanders entrusted with great military responsibility. Unfortunately, the operating environment has now changed radically from that which prevailed during their formative years. This unfortunately makes them highly susceptible to very persuasive and convincing sales talk from communication contractors. Why would you NOT buy an IO program from a company that, say, boosted sales of a particular car by 30 percent? Superficially, it seems logical, but the nuance of the type of communication, and the precise effect sought, is lost on busy military people who have no background in this area. The simple fact is that a U.S. consumer has probably already made the decision to buy a new car—the behavioral change has been self-enacted. The marketer's task is now only to differentiate their product from all others, which they may do via cost or associating it with some celebrity endorsement—the SUV that George Clooney drives, for example. But what about crises or conflict situations where the audience has not made the behavioral change, as indeed in Afghanistan, because it does not like any of the options available? No amount of marketing will make **that** product attractive. As Lieutenant Colonel Cook notes:

> the [US] COIN strategy assumes the [Afghan] people will either support the government or the Taliban. . . . . The truth is, there is a third choice that seriously undermines the coalition's strategy: most Afghans, if freely given the choice, will support neither.[93]

In short, senior U.S. figures both inside and outside the military have been encouraged by large contractors to pay a lot of money that try to sell to Afghans a "vision" of the country that fails to connect utterly with the reality of their lives. Yet in almost every problem that confronts the United States and its allies, it is behavior that must be addressed—in most instances, the IO objective set does not presuppose any attitudinal change. The motivations for the undesired behavior will only be found through robust TAA—listening, observing, and understanding—but it appears in many instances that this vital step has, at best, been **superficial and, at worst, completely absent.** Despite having not seen the full range of U.S. IO programs over the last 11 years (although the author has seen a very great many), it is possible to offer an opinion with some certainty because, had TAA been properly undertaken, the DoD would have been able to show Congressional Oversight Committees the MOE—and it is quite apparent from congressional comments that this simply has not happened. The industry has made millions from the U.S. Government but, in fact, has done the cause of IO a great disservice by promising, or at least suggesting, solutions that were never more than aspirational.

Any U.S. decision to draw down costs for IO funding would therefore be entirely understandable in the face of apparent failure over the last few years. But once again, this does not denote a failure of IO as a concept, but of its implementation. The author contends that the United States must rethink its whole approach to IO, in particular the methodologies and contractors it employs, but it **must not** reduce the program — indeed, just the opposite. It must reinvigorate it, but with intelligent customers and contractors who can work in the areas of behaviors, not attitudes, properly deliver, and adapt quickly, to changing circumstances. This is not a new or revolutionary proposition. A search of the U.S. Combined Arms Research Library reveals a deep and rich seam of thinking by U.S. military students at staff colleges. For example, Lieutenant Colonel Barrett Burns, U.S. Army, wrote his staff college dissertation on using social influence techniques in ISAF; Major Joseph Cox, U.S. Army, wrote his thesis on the failure of resourcing IO in Iraq and Afghanistan; and Major Alfred Roach, U.S. Army, wrote about the problems of using out-dated messaging models.

As a senior U.S. State Department official told the UK's Advanced Command and Staff Course, "America must learn to do more with less."[94] Huge amounts of U.S. taxpayer monies have been spent on U.S. information activities since 2001. In 2002, the Pew research Global Attitudes Study revealed that:

> Since 2000, favorability ratings for the U.S. have fallen in 19 of the 27 countries where trend benchmarks are

available. . . . [T]rue dislike, if not hatred, of America is concentrated in the Muslim nations of the Middle East and in Central Asia, today's areas of greatest conflict.[95]

In 2011, the same organization reported that:

The rise of pro-democracy movements has not led to an improvement in America's image in the region. Instead, in key Arab nations and in other predominantly Muslim countries, views of the U.S. remain negative, as they have been for nearly a decade. Indeed, in Jordan, Turkey and Pakistan, views are even more negative than they were one year ago. . . . Moreover, many of the concerns that have driven animosity toward the U.S. in recent years are still present — a perception that the U.S. acts unilaterally, opposition to the war on terror, and fears of America as a military threat. And in countries such as Jordan, Lebanon, and Pakistan, most say their own governments cooperate too much with the U.S.[96]

In a 2012 survey of opinion in Pakistan, Pew Research reported that:

Roughly three-in-four Pakistanis (74%) consider the U.S. an enemy, up from 69% last year and 64% three years ago. And President Obama is held in exceedingly low regard.[97]

While trying to achieve more with less is an admirable idea, these survey trends suggest that, in this important area, the United States has actually achieved **less** with **more** and, in any event, in focusing on attitudes, may actually be trying to do the wrong thing. It seems time for a fundamental rethink in tactics and contractors.

RECOMMENDATIONS

A summary of recommendations follows.

- SC and IO are force multipliers. Their operation has become hugely bureaucratic and cumbersome; streamlining them for efficiency makes eminent sense, cutting them does not.
- The United States needs to stop attempting to transplant ideas from civilian marketing and advertising into conflict environments. They do not work and may even be counterproductive. Employ specialists, not commercial communication and advertising companies.
- There are two components to an influence campaign — profiling the audience (TAA) and actually influencing the audience. Historically, neither has been performed well. Follow some basic rules:
  - TAA is the *sine qua non* of IO and SC; without it you rely upon luck and may even do more damage than doing nothing.
  - TAA is not polling; the best TAA is undertaken in-country through qualitative research techniques.
  - If the TAA indicates that attitudinal change is all that is required to motivate an audience, then an attitudinal campaign is sufficient. However, more often than not, attitudinal change is not enough to motivate a change of behavior. Always focus on the behavioral outcome — not the attitudinal transition.
  - Communication may only be a **part** of the behavioral change program — the TAA will indicate whether this is the case. Embrace the idea of full-spectrum targeting and integrate at the strategic and operational levels.

- MOE is a measurement of the change which has occurred in an audience group, in line with the mission's objectives. It can only be measured against a previously measured baseline—requiring TAA to happen in advance.
- DoD might consider a collaborative arrangement with other SC and IO focused nations, specifically the UK, Australia, and Canada, for the sharing of best practice and joint funding of large projects. Look beyond the U.S. primes for best practice.
- Other countries such as China and Russia are taking IO very seriously indeed. They appear agile and adapt quickly to changing circumstances. The United Staates needs to be monitoring and understanding their processes. The three warfares policy potentially provides China with far greater capability than just cyber attack.
- The United States needs to examine its bureaucracy and ask fundamental questions:
  - Is it currently wed to contractors who can do what is required? If not, change it . . . and them!
  - Is it fit and agile enough to deal with 21st century challenges? If not, change it.[98]

ENDNOTES

1. If, indeed, there was one single point in a sectarian conflict that was never predicted but which was ignited in the February 2006 bombing of the Shiite Samarra Mosque. Events such as the Sunni tribal "Anbar awakening" were also never predicted.

2. David Gompert and John Gordon, *War by Other Means: Building Complete and Balanced Capabilities for Counterinsurgency*, Washington, DC: Rand Corporation, 2007.

3. John MacKinlay, *The Insurgent Archipelago*, London, UK: C. Hurst & Co. 2009.

4. David Kilcullen, *The Accidental Guerrilla: Fighting Small Wars in the Midst of a Big One,* London, UK: C. Hurst & Co. 2011.

5. Rupert Smith, *The Utility of Force: The Art of War in the Modern World,* London, UK: Penguin, 2006.

6. Dale Andrade and James Willbanks, "CORDS/Phoenix. Counterinsurgency Lessons from Vietnam for the Future," *Military Review*, March/April 2006, pp. 77–91.

7. See *smallwarsjournal.com/jrnl/art/war-is-about-killing-and-destruction.*

8. John Cook, *Afghanistan: The Perfect Failure. A War Doomed by the Coalition's Strategies, Policies and Political Correctness,* Bloomington, IL: Xlibris Press, 2012.

9. Tom Vandenbrook, "U.S. 'info ops' programs dubious, costly," *USA Today,* February 29, 2012.

10. Tom Vandenbook, "DoD's overseas propaganda plan raises concerns," *USA Today,* November 19, 2012.

11. *Ibid.*

12. Arturo Munoz, *"US Military Information Operations in Afghanistan 2001-2010,"* available from *www.rand.org/pubs/monographs/2012/RAND_MG1060.pdf.*

13. George Little, *"Communication Syncronisation – A Local Coordination Process,"* Memorandum from George Little to U.S. Commanders of Combatant Commands (CCDR), November 28, 2012.

14. See *www.linkedin.com/groupItem?view=&gid=816587&type=member&item=191319744&commentID=108441156&qid=93cc9240-f126-423a-be6c-b14bd3ead64b&goback=.gmp_816587.*

15. Rosa Brooks, "*Confessions of a Strategic Communicator. Tales from Inside the Pentagon's Message Machine,*"available from *www.foreignpolicy.com/articles/2012/12/06/confessions_of_a_strategic_communicator.*

16. See *www.linkedin.com/groups/Pentagon-Drops-Strategic-Communication-putting-816587%2ES%2E192572946?qid=97ce05e0-c137-4f4f-84b2-a4c5121e04c8&trk=group_items_see_more-0-b-ttl.*

17. *Joint Publication (JP) 3-13, Information Operations,* Washington, DC: U.S. Department of Defense, November 27, 2012.

18. *JP 1-02, DOD Dictionary of Military and Associated Terms,* Washington, DC: U.S. Department of Defense, November 8, 2010, as amended through April 15, 2013.

19. "*Examination of Wedding dowries as a means of behavioral influence,*" A proposal by the International Council on Security and Development (ICOS) for the International Security and Assistance Force (ISAF) May 1, 2011.

20. See *abcnews.go.com/International/deadly-anti-us-riots-pakistan-obamas-ad-denouncing/story?id=17291751.*

21. The UK government defines "intelligent customers" as "The capability of the organisation to have a clear understanding and knowledge of the product or service being supplied," available from *www.hse.gov.uk/humanfactors/topics/customers.htm.*

22. Lieutenant General William B Caldwell IV, "Towards Transition," *Defence Management Journal,* Issue 51, undated, available from *www.defencemanagement.com/article.asp?id=464&content_name=Overview&article=15917.*

23. See *thehill.com/blogs/blog-briefing-room/news/63121-crs-calculates-cost-of-us-troop-presence-in-afghanistan.*

24. See *www.thesun.co.uk/sol/homepage/news/4481938/Official-Casualties-soaring-in-20mph-zones.html.*

25. Kim Gragin and Scott Gerwehr, "Dissuading Terror, Strategic Influence and the Struggle Against Terrorism," Washington, DC: The RAND Corporation, 2005.

26. William Hutchinson and Matthew Warren, "Influence Operations and Behavioural Change," Paper prepared for the "European Conference On Information Warfare and Security," Thessalonica, Greece, July 2012.

27. The unfortunate soldier was killed before such assets could be deployed.

28. See *www.sada-e-azadi.net*.

29. Cook, p. 201.

30. See *csc.asu.edu/wp-content/uploads/pdf/121.pdf*.

31. Pertinent examples include Richard LaPiere, "Attitudes Versus Actions," *Social Forces Journal*, 1934; and Martin Fishbein and Icek Azjen, a 1947 study re-published in *Predicting & Changing Behavior: The Reasoned Action Approach,* New York: Psychology Press, 2009.

32. Richard Holbrooke, "Get the Message Out," *The Washington Post*, October 28, 2001, p. B07.

33. Hutchinson and Warren.

34. See *www.rand.org/pubs/monographs/MG607.html*.

35. Al Ries and Jack Trout, *Positioning: The Battle for Your Mind,* New York: McGraw-Hill, 2000.

36. Richard Wike, "*Wait – You still don't like us?*" Pew Global Attitude Project, Washington, DC, available from *www.pewglobal. org/2012/09/19/wait-you-still-dont-like-us/*.

37. A Kurdish Muslim, Sala-ad Din, founded the Ayyubid dynasty, ruling over lands today known as Egypt, Syria, Iraq, and parts of Saudi Arabia and Yemen.

38. R. H. Crossman OBE MP, "Psychological Warfare in World War Two to the Royal United Services Institute," *RUSI Journal*, Vol. XCVII, No. 587, August 1952.

39. Martin F. Herz, "Some Psychological Lessons from Leaflet Propaganda in World War II," *The Public Opinion Quarterly*, Vol. 13, No. 3, Autumn, 1949, pp. 471-486.

40. Karl Eikenberry, "There is hope yet for Afghanistan," *The Financial Times*, November 20, 2012.

41. See *www.instituteofcustomerservice.com/167-7669/UK-Customer-Satisfaction-Index-Results-July-2011.html*.

42. Alan Travis, "Police in Britain Deemed Untrustworthy Compared with Europe, Says Study," *The Guardian Newspaper*, December 12, 2011.

43. U.S. Department of Justice, "*Satisfaction with Police – What Matters?*" Washington, DC: Department of Justice, available from *www.ncjrs.gov/pdffiles1/nij/194077.pdf*.

44. A huge number of polls and surveys are undertaken in Afghanistan, and their results can be found all over the Internet: from large polling organizations employed by ISAF through to indivisible national initiatives to measure their individual performance. But just how reliable is the science of surveys? A significant determinant of the validity of polling is the manner in which the question is phrased and presented. But assuming this is done consistently across all polled groups, the reality of surveys is that they will only ever tell you what the polled thought about something at a particular point in time. Surveys and polling are highly temporal and closely related attitudinal.

45. See *www.edge.org/*.

46. James Prochaska, Carlo DiClemente, and John Norcross, "In Search of How People Change. Applications to Addictive Behaviors," *American Psychologist*, Vol. 47, No. 9, 1992, pp. 1102-1114.

47. Department of Defense Appropriations Bill; Report of the Committee on Appropriations, Washington, DC: U.S. Department of Defense, 2010, p. 67.

48. Office of the Secretary State for Defense, *"Military Power of the People's Republic of China 2008: Annual Report to Congress,"* Washington, DC: U.S. Department of Defense, 2008.

49. Office of the Secretary of State for Defense *"Military and Security Developments Involving the People's Republic of China, Annual Report to Congress,"* Washington, DC: U.S. Department of Defense, 2011.

50. Timothy A Walton, *"China's Three Warfares,"* Herndon, VA: Delex Consulting, January 18, 2012.

51. *Ibid.*

52. Timothy Thomas, *"Dragon Bytes,"* Ft. Leavenworth, KS: Foreign Military Studies Office, 2004, p. 98.

53. Rear Admiral Yang Yi, Chinese Navy, Interview with the BBC, available from *www.bbc.co.uk/news/world-asia-china-19710040.*

54. See *www.foreignpolicy.com/articles/2012/09/26/the_calm_before_the_storm?page=0,2.*

55. Christopher Williams, "Pentagon confirms Beijing's anti-satellite laser. Wi jammin', and I hope Yu like jammin' too," *The Register,* October 6, 2006.

56. See *www.cryptome.org/cuw.htm#Part%20Two.*

57. Adam Segal, "China's Twitter War," *Asia Unbound*, March 22, 2012.

58. Alex Michael, *"Cyber Probing: The Politicisation of Virtual Attack,"* Swindon, UK: UK Defence Academy, September 2010.

59. See *www.weibo.com.*

60. Timothy Thomas, *"Comparing US, Russian and Chinese IO Concepts,"* Ft. Leavenworth, KS: Foreign Military Studies Office, 2004.

61. Mark Lloyd, *The Art of Military Deception,* London, UK: Pen and Sword Books, 1997, p. 115.

62. Brian Daily and Patrick Parker, *"Soviet Strategic Deception,"* London, UK: The Free Press, 1987, p. 294.

63. *Ibid.*

64. Timothy Thomas, "Russia's Reflexive Control Theory & The Military," *The Journal of Slavic & Military Studies,* Vol. 17, London, UK: Frank Cass, 2004, pp. 237–256.

65. See *www.au.af.mil/info-ops/perception.htm#reflexive.*

66. Timothy Thomas, *"The Russian View Of Information War,"* Ft. Leavenworth, KS, Foreign Military Studies Office, 2000; Michael Crutcher, *"The Russian Armed Forces at the Dawn of the Millennium,"* Carlisle, PA: U.S. Army War College, Carlisle, 2000.

67. *Ibid.*

68. *Ibid.*

69. *Ibid.*

70. Stephen Cimbala, *"Military Persuasion in War and Policy: The Power of Soft,"* Westport, CT: Praeger Press, 2002, p. 23.

71. A reference, perhaps, to the large number of western intellectuals who sympathized with the Soviet Union and, in some cases, actively spied for it.

72. Charles Blandy, *"Provocation, Deception, Entrapment: The Russo-Georgian Five Day War,"* ARAG Paper 09/01, Swindon, UK: UK Defense Academy, 2009.

73. Author interview with Steve Tatham/Charles Blandy, Swindon, UK: UK Defence Academy, March 31, 2009.

74. Charles Blandy, "Georgia & Russia: A Further Deterioration in Relations," ARAG paper, Swindon, UK: UK Defense Academy, August 22, 2008.

75. "Russian Strategic/Operational Influence Activities in Georgia 2008," Briefing to NATO Senior Officers Info Ops Orientation Course, September 23, 2010.

76. Brooks.

77. See *www.gao.gov/new.items/d07904.pdf*.

78. Robert Zoellick, *"Whither China: From Membership to Responsibility?"* Vol. 16, No. 4, Washington, DC: National Bureau of Asian Research, December 2005.

79. Stephen Olsen and Clyde Prestowitz, "The Evolving Role of China in International Institutions," prepared for The U.S.-China Economic and Security Review Commission, January 2011.

80. Remarks of Deputy Chief of Mission to London Barbara J. Stephenson to the UK Advanced Command and Staff Course, Swindon, UK, February 20, 2013.

81. *Ibid.*

82. David Betz, *Cyberpower and International Security*, Foreign Policy Research Institute Newsletter, June 2012.

83. Munoz.

84. *Redefining Information Warfare Boundaries For An Army In A Wireless World*, Santa Monica, CA: Rand Corporation, 2013, available from *www.rand.org/pubs/monographs/mg1113.html*.

85. See *usatoday30.usatoday.com/news/military/story/2012-06-19/leonie-pentagon-contracts/55696176/1*.

86. Munoz.

87. See *www.cbpp.org/cms/index.cfm?fa=view&id=1258*.

88. See *tv.msnbc.com/2013/01/07/americans-are-ready-for-sensible-reduction-in-military-spending/*.

89. Lecture to UK Advanced Command and Staff Course, UK Defence Academy, Swindon, UK, Febuary 2013.

90. Matt Cavanagh, "Ministerial Decision Making in the Run up to the Helmand Deployment," *RUSI Journal*, May/June 2012.

91. Michael Hastings, *The Operators: The Wild and Terrifying Inside Story of America's War in Afghanistan*, London, UK: Orion Press, 2012.

92. See *www.dailymail.co.uk/news/article-2046334/Afghanistan-war-10th-anniversary-invasion-half-way-there.html*.

93. Cook.

94. Remarks of Deputy Chief of Mission to London Barbara J. Stephenson to the UK Advanced Command and Staff Course.

95. *Obama's Challenge in the Muslim World. Arab Spring Fails to improve US Image,* Washington, DC: Pew Research Global Attitudes Project, released May 17, 2011.

96. *Ibid.*

97. 2012 Global Attitudes Survey, Pew Research Global Attitudes Project.

98. Evgeny Morozov, "What do They Teach at the Kremlin School of Bloggers," *Foreign Policy* website available from *neteffect.foreignpolicy.com/posts/2009/05/26/what_do_they_teach_at_kremlins_school_of_bloggers*.